Some Understood

Poems for reflection and meditation

edited by Alison Morgan

"Poetry is not an end in itself but in the service of life;
of what use are poems, or any other works of art, unless
to enable human lives to be lived with insight of a deeper kind,
with more sensitive feelings, more intense sense of the beautiful,
with deeper understanding?"

Kathleen Raine

The Mathetes Trust 2017

ISBN 978-1-912124-99-2

Published by The Mathetes Trust
www.mathetestrust.org

March 2017

Foreword

Something Understood is a sequel to an earlier collection, *Distilling Life*, published in 2012. We were delighted by the ways in which people used *Distilling Life* – some for their own reflection and meditation, some to give as presents, some to share with book groups, some to read aloud in public settings. The guiding principle of this second anthology has been the same as that of the first – to help people pause awhile in the flurry of life, take stock, and allow the words of others to nourish their own emotional and spiritual lives.

As before, the poems are chosen from a wide variety of historical periods and perspectives, but they are arranged in a different way. Instead of following a meandering path designed as a continuous spiritual journey, the poems of *Something Understood* are arranged in five sections, each of which tackles one of the major aspects of human experience: Seeing, Living, Loving, Trusting and Dying. For the first time, some prose selections are included. You may prefer to read the poems in the quiet of your own room, or you may wish to use them as a gateway to discussion with others – it's not always easy to share deep things, and yet our wellbeing so often depends on our ability to do so.

The title comes, of course, from the well-known 17th century poem on prayer by George Herbert. It expresses the desire to penetrate beyond the surface of things, to pause, take stock and allow reality to become real in our own jumbled lives; to grasp the things that matter, and in opening ourselves to moments somehow to glimpse eternity. We live in a muddled and confusing world; but if the world, and our lives within the world, bear the scars of pain, the scars of alienation from God, so also they bear the marks of the love and the power which invite us to go deeper, and so prepare us for the coming of a reality bigger than ourselves, one which will both complete and transcend our present experience. For the time being, life is all around us, if only we have the eyes to see it and the courage to respond to it.

And that, I think, is why we read poetry. Kathleen Raine puts it well when she observes that "Poetry is not an end in itself but in the service of life; of what use are poems, or any other works of art, unless to enable human lives to be lived with insight of a deeper kind, with more sensitive feelings, more intense sense of the beautiful, with deeper understanding?"

It is our hope that this volume will help you to do that.

Alison Morgan, Wells, March 2017

Something Understood

Why are we reading, if not in hope of beauty laid bare, life heightened and its deepest mystery probed? Can the writer isolate and vivify all in experience that most deeply engages our intellects and our hearts? Can the writer renew our hope for literary forms? Why are we reading if not in hope that the writer will magnify and dramatize our days, will illuminate and inspire us with wisdom, courage, and the possibility of meaning- fulness, and will press upon our minds the deepest mysteries, so we may feel again their majesty and power? What do we ever know that is higher than that power which, from time to time, seizes our lives, and reveals us startlingly to ourselves as creatures set down here bewildered? Why does death so catch us by surprise, and why love? We still and always want waking. We should amass half dressed in long lines like tribesmen and shake gourds at each other, to wake up; instead we watch television and miss the show.

Annie Dillard

SOMETHING UNDERSTOOD
Contents

I : SEEING

II : LIVING

III : LOVING

IV : TRUSTING

V : DYING

I : Seeing

This is the moment which I call epiphany. First we recognise that the object is one integral thing, then we recognise that it is an organized composite structure, a thing in fact: finally, when the relation of the parts is exquisite, when the parts are adjusted to the special point, we recognize that it is that thing which it is. Its soul, its whatness, leaps to us from the vestment of its appearance. The soul of the commonest object, the structure of which is so adjusted, seems to us radiant. The object achieves its epiphany.

James Joyce

Moses at the Burning Bush

Moses was keeping the flock of his father-in-law Jethro, the priest of Midian; he led his flock beyond the wilderness, and came to Horeb, the mountain of God. There the angel of the LORD appeared to him in a flame of fire out of a bush; he looked, and the bush was blazing, yet it was not consumed. Then Moses said, 'I must turn aside and look at this great sight, and see why the bush is not burned up.' When the LORD saw that he had turned aside to see, God called to him out of the bush, 'Moses, Moses!' And he said, 'Here I am.' Then he said, 'Come no closer! Remove the sandals from your feet, for the place on which you are standing is holy ground.' He said further, 'I am the God of your father, the God of Abraham, the God of Isaac, and the God of Jacob.' And Moses hid his face, for he was afraid to look at God.

Exodus 3.1-6

I find you, Lord, in all Things

I find you, Lord, in all Things and in all
my fellow creatures, pulsing with your life;
as a tiny seed you sleep in what is small
and in the vast you vastly yield yourself.

The wondrous game that power plays with Things
is to move in such submission through the world:
groping in roots and growing thick in trunks
and in treetops like a rising from the dead.

Rainer Maria Rilke

Psalm 8

O LORD, our Sovereign,
   how majestic is your name in all the earth!
You have set your glory above the heavens.
Out of the mouths of babes and infants
   you have founded a bulwark because of your foes,
   to silence the enemy and the avenger.
When I look at your heavens, the work of your fingers,
   the moon and the stars that you have established;
what are human beings that you are mindful of them,
   mortals that you care for them?
Yet you have made them a little lower than God,
   and crowned them with glory and honour.
You have given them dominion over the works of your hands;
   you have put all things under their feet,
all sheep and oxen,
   and also the beasts of the field,
the birds of the air, and the fish of the sea,
   whatever passes along the paths of the seas.
O LORD, our Sovereign,
   how majestic is your name in all the earth!

King David

A Thicket in Lleyn

This is a thoroughfare for migrants, warblers in spring, thrushes in autumn. Once on a day in October, after the gales had stripped it, it was alive with goldcrests. The air purred with their small wings. To look up was to see the twigs re-leafed with their bodies. Everywhere their needle-sharp cries stitched at the silence. Was I invisible? Their seed-bright eyes regarded me from three feet off. Had I put forth an arm, they might have perched on it. I became a tree, part of that bare spinney where silently the light was splintered, and for a timeless moment the birds thronged me, filigreeing me with shadow, moving to an immemorial rhythm on their way south.

Then suddenly they were gone, leaving other realities to return: the rustle of the making tide, the tick of the moisture, the blinking of the pool's eye as the air flicked it; and lastly myself. Where had I been? Who was I? What did it all mean? While it was happening, I was not. Now that the birds had gone, here I was once again.

No, while the experience lasted, I was absent or in abeyance. It was when I returned to myself that I realized that I was other, more than the experience, able to stand back and comprehend it by means of the imagination, and so by this act of creation to recognize myself not as lived by, but as part of the infinite I AM.

R S Thomas

A Thicket in Lleyn

I was no tree walking.
I was still. They ignored me,
the birds, the migrants
on their way south. They re-leafed
the trees, budding them
with their notes. They filtered through
the boughs like sunlight,
looked at me from three feet
off, their eyes blackberry bright.,
not seeing me, not detaching me
from the withies, where I was
caged and they free.
                    They would have perched
on me, had I had nourishment
in my fissures. As it was
they netted me in their shadows,
brushed me with sound, feathering the arrows
of their own bows, and were gone,
leaving me to reflect on the answer
to a question I had not asked.
'A repetition in time of the eternal
I AM.' Say it. Don't be shy.
Escape from your mortal cage
in thought. Your migrations will never
be over. Between two truths
there is only the mind to fly with.
Navigate by such stars as are not
leaves falling from life's
deciduous tree, but spray from the fountain
of the imagination, endlessly
replenishing itself out of its own waters.

R S Thomas

Loveliest of trees

Loveliest of trees, the cherry now
Is hung with bloom along the bough,
And stands about the woodland ride
Wearing white for Eastertide.

Now, of my threescore years and ten,
Twenty will not come again,
And take from seventy springs a score,
It only leaves me fifty more.

And since to look at things in bloom
Fifty springs are little room,
About the woodlands I will go
To see the cherry hung with snow.

A. E. Housman

The Eternal Now

We forget that life can only be defined in the present tense; it *is*, and
it is *now*, and that nowness has become so vivid to me that I'm
almost serene. I can celebrate life. Below my window the blossom is
out in full. It's a plum tree; and instead of saying, 'Oh, that's nice
blossom', looking at it through the window it is the whitest, frothiest,
blossomest blossom there ever could be. And I can *see* it; and things
are both more trivial than they ever were and more important than
they ever were, and the difference between the trivial and the
important doesn't seem to matter, but the nowness of everything is
absolutely wondrous.

Dennis Potter

as he contemplated his approaching death
from an interview with Melvyn Bragg, Channel 4, April 1994

Home-Thoughts, from Abroad

Oh, to be in England
Now that April's there,
And whoever wakes in England
Sees, some morning, unaware,
That the lowest boughs and the brushwood sheaf
Round the elm-tree bole are in tiny leaf,
While the chaffinch sings on the orchard bough
In England – now!

And after April, when May follows,
And the whitethroat builds, and all the swallows!
Hark, where my blossomed pear-tree in the hedge
Leans to the field and scatters on the clover
Blossoms and dewdrops – at the bent spray's edge –
That's the wise thrush; he sings each song twice over,
Lest you should think he never could recapture
The first fine careless rapture!
And though the fields look rough with hoary dew,
All will be gay when noontide wakes anew
The buttercups, the little children's dower
– Far brighter than this gaudy melon-flower!

Robert Browning

Blackbird in Fulham

A John the Baptist bird which comes before
The light, chooses an aerial
Toothed like a garden rake, puts a prong at each shoulder,
Opens its beak and becomes a thurifer
Blessing dark above dank holes between the houses,
Sleek patios or rag-and-weed-choked messes.

Too aboriginal to notice these,
Its concentration is on resonance
Which excavates in sleepers memories
Long overgrown or expensively paved-over,
Of innocence unmawkish, love robust.
Its sole belief, that light will come at last.

The point is proved and, casual, it flies elsewhere
To sing more distantly, as though its tune
Is left behind imprinted on the air,
Still legible, though this the second carbon.
And puzzled wakers lie and listen hard
To something moving in their minds' backyard.

P J Kavanagh

Some Solitude

To be alone just as I often was
When small, before the name of solitude
Or loneliness impinged on what I did,
To be alone, my mind among the stars,
My hands brushing the lavender and herbs,
My senses clear of smoke and dirt and all
Intrusions – is this begging far too much?
Is it selfish when I go away,
Many miles sometimes,
Sometimes for only an hour when I reflect
And tilt my head to memorize the shapes
Of altering clouds in sudden heat-wave this
Whole of April offered? I think not
For in the solitude when I become
One with birdsong, shifts of winds, the slant
Of sun across the land and hill at noon
I can achieve no peace but some wise state
In which I find both pleasure and renewal,
Knowledge unknown to books, feelings unspoilt
By passion or sensation's touch. So long
As this sometimes can lead to mines the spirit
Finds its own gold in and then offers it back
To one or two or who knows what's the count,
Then there's no need to justify my purpose,
I draw away to be of use, discover
How spirit speaks to spirit, time's no matter
And none knows what amount.

Elizabeth Jennings

A Rose for Winter

At first there was nothing – a profound blue darkness running deep, laced by skeins of starlight and pale phosphorescent flashes. This four o'clock hour was a moment of utter silence, the indrawn breath of dark, the absolute, trance-like balance between night and day.

Then, when it seemed that nothing would ever move or live or know the light again, a sudden hot wind would run over the invisible water. It was like a fore-blast of the turning world, an intimation that its rocks and seas and surfaces still stirred against the sun. One strained one's eyes, scarce breathing, searching for a sign.

Presently it came. Far in the east at last the horizon hardened, an imperceptible line dividing sky and sea, sharp as a diamond cut on glass. A dark bubble of cloud revealed itself, warmed slowly, flushing from within like a seed growing, a kernel ripening, a clinker hot with a locked-in fire.

Gradually the cloud throbbed red with light, then suddenly caught the still unrisen sun and burst like an expanding bomb. Flares and streamers began to fall into the sea, setting all things on fire.

After the long unthinking darkness everything now began to happen at once. The stars snapped shut, the sky bled green, vermilion tides ran over the water, the hills around took on the colour of firebrick, and the great sun drew himself at last raw and dripping from the waves.

Scarlet, purple and clinker-blue, the morning, smelling of thyme and goats, of charcoal, splintered rock and man's long sojourn around this lake, returned with a calling of dogs, the cough of asses and the hoarse speech of the fishermen going down to the working sea.

Laurie Lee

On The Scribbled Wall

On the scribbled wall
that shades the scattered benches
the arch of the sky appears
complete.

Who now remembers the wildfire that burned
hot and strong
through the veins of the world; – in cold rest
now the shapes lie, scattered, opaque.

Tomorrow I'll see the quays again
and the wall and the familiar road.
In the future that opens up, the mornings
are moored like boats in the harbour.

Eugenio Montale

translated by Alison Morgan

Autumn

I love the fitful gust that shakes
  The casement all the day,
And from the mossy elm tree takes
  The faded leaves away,
Twirling them by the window pane
With thousand others down the lane.

I love to see the shaking twig
  Dance till the shut of eve,
The sparrow on the cottage rig,
  Whose chirp would make believe
That Spring was just now flirting by
In Summer's lap with flowers to lie.

I love to see the cottage smoke
  Curl upwards through the trees,
The pigeons nestled round the cote
  On November days like these;
The cock upon the dunghill crowing,
The mill sails on the heath a-going.

The feather from the raven's breast
  Falls on the stubble lea
The acorns near the old crow's nest
  Drop pattering down the tree
The grunting pigs that wait for all
Scramble and hurry where they fall.

John Clare

On Lake Nicaragua

Slow cargo-launch, midnight, mid-lake,
bound from San Miguelito to Granada.
The lights ahead not yet in sight,
the dwindling ones behind completely gone.
Only the stars
(the mast a finger pointing to the Seven Sisters)
and the moon, rising above Chontales.

Another launch (just one red light) goes by
and sinks into the night.
We, for them:
another red light sinking in the night...
And I, watching the stars, lying on the deck
between bunches of bananas and Chontales cheeses,
wonder: perhaps there's one that is an earth like ours
and someone's watching me (watching the stars)
from another launch, on another night, on another lake.

Ernesto Cardenal

Translated By Ernesto Cardenal And Robert Pring-Mill

The Word

Down near the bottom
of the crossed-out list
of things you have to do today,

between "green thread"
and "broccoli," you find
that you have penciled "sunlight."

Resting on the page, the word
is beautiful. It touches you
as if you had a friend

and sunlight were a present
he had sent from someplace distant
as this morning – to cheer you up,

and to remind you that,
among your duties, pleasure
is a thing

that also needs accomplishing.
Do you remember?
that time and light are kinds

of love, and love
is no less practical
than a coffee grinder

or a safe spare tire?
Tomorrow you may be utterly
without a clue,

but today you get a telegram
from the heart in exile,
proclaiming that the kingdom

still exists,
the king and queen alive,
still speaking to their children,

– to any one among them
who can find the time
to sit out in the sun and listen.

Tony Hoagland

March

On a morning like this one
when all the quiet jewels of God are on display
(the rose-quartz sky behind the brazen oak,
the willow with fronds like amber in the gentle sun)
one might expect birdsong
(the careful aria of the songthrush,
the robin small in the poplars' filigree,
the sleek green woodpecker proud on the lawn)
but not like this:
three fat ducks waddle quacking into view.
Yet see: the sun plays on their shining necks,
the morning laughs loudest in their bright feet,
the day quickens.

Katy Morgan

Railways

The railways created as much as they inadvertently destroyed, but of a totally different kind. The great gashes they inflicted on the landscape in their cuttings and embankments healed over, and wild flowers grew abundantly once more. Going down to the south-west in spring, the cuttings through Somerset and Devon sparkle with primroses. Even in Clare's own country, the railway has been absorbed into the landscape, and one can enjoy the consequent pleasure of trundling through Rutland in a stopping-train on a fine summer morning: the barley fields shaking in the wind, the slow sedgy streams with their willows shading meditative cattle, the elegant limestone spires across the meadows, the early Victorian stations built of the sheep-grey Ketton stone and still unaltered, the warm brown roofs of the villages half buried in the trees, and the summer light flashing everywhere. True that the railway did not invent much of this beauty, but it gave us new vistas of it.

W S Hoskins

Adlestrop

Yes, I remember Adlestrop –
The name, because one afternoon
Of heat the express-train drew up there
Unwontedly. It was late June.

The steam hissed. Someone cleared his throat.
No one left and no one came
On the bare platform. What I saw
Was Adlestrop – only the name

And willows, willow-herb, and grass,
And meadowsweet, and haycocks dry,
No whit less still and lonely fair
Than the high cloudlets in the sky.

And for that minute a blackbird sang
Close by, and round him, mistier,
Farther and farther, all the birds
Of Oxfordshire and Gloucestershire.

Edward Thomas

Adlestrop

And now, only the name is left
Brown and white, as a bus stop sign
Stone twisting leaves of autumn gold
Shared memories, now yours, now mine.

Jackdaws called. Someone unlocked the church.
We walked across the fields and saw
Nothing there. No one left and no one came
And what we found was little more

Than memories of mist and flower
An old station building, rusting stock
A keep out sign. And then it rained
And inside my heart was burst a lock

Of sadness, but then of cloudfree peace
For still they sang, those birds – not now
In time-stilled layers, but a single voice:
A robin, dripping golden dreams from hidden bough.

Alison Morgan

October

Skies, big skies, careening over in the wind;
great shoals of cloud pitching and jostling
in their rush to be anywhere other than here.

You hesitate on your doorstep, glance up
and something tugs in your chest, rips free like a leaf
and is sucked up and away. Everything's

finished here: raw-boned sycamores,
fields scalped and sodden. The houses are shut
and dustbins roll in their own filth in the street.

So you would take your chances, risk it all...
You stand for a moment with the keys in your hand
feeling the pull of the sky and the moment passing.

Jean Sprackland

As Kingfishers Catch Fire

As kingfishers catch fire, dragonflies draw flame;
As tumbled over rim in roundy wells
Stones ring; like each tucked string tells, each hung bell's
Bow swung finds tongue to fling out broad its name;
Each mortal thing does one thing and the same:
Deals out that being indoors each one dwells;
Selves – goes itself; *myself* it speaks and spells,
Crying *Whát I dó is me: for that I came.*

Í say móre: the just man justices;
Keeps gráce: thát keeps all his goings graces;
Acts in God's eye what in God's eye he is –
Chríst – for Christ plays in ten thousand places,
Lovely in limbs, and lovely in eyes not his
To the Father through the features of men's faces.

Gerard Manley Hopkins

The Peregrine

The peregrine was restless and wild as I followed him across the soaking ploughland clay. He flickered lightly ahead of me in the driving rain, flitting from bush to post, from post to fence, from fence to overhead wire... The rain stopped, the sky cleared, and the hawk began to fly faster. At two o'clock he raced away to the east through snaking lariats of starlings. Effortlessly he climbed above them, red-gold shining above black. They ringed up in pursuit, and he dipped neatly beneath them. Beyond the river he swept down to ground level and the starlings rose steeply up like spray from a breaking wave. They could not overtake him. He was running free, wind flowing from the curves of his wings like water from the back of a diving otter. ... Running across fields, clambering over gates, cycling along lanes, I followed at my own poor speed. Fortunately he did not get too far ahead, for he paused to chase every flock of birds he saw. They were not serious attacks; he was not yet hunting; it was like a puppy frisking after butterflies. Fieldfares, lapwings, gulls, and golden plover, were scattered, and driven, and goaded into panic. Rooks, jackdaws, sparrows, and skylarks, were threshed up from the furrows and flung about like dead leaves. The whole sky hissed and rained with birds. And with each rush, and plunge, and zigzagging pursuit, his playfulness ebbed away and his hunger grew. He climbed above the hills, looking for sport among the spiky orchards and the moss-green oak woods. Starlings rose into the sky like black searchlight beams, and wavered aimlessly about, seeking the hawk. Woodpigeons began to come back from the east like the survivors of a battle, flying low across the fields. There were thousands of them feeding on acorns in the woods, and the hawk had found them. From every wood and covert, as far as I could see, flock after flock went roaring up into the sky, keeping very close, circling and swirling like dunlin. ... The peregrine was clearing the entire hill of its pigeons, stooping at each wood in turn, sweeping along the rides, flicking between the trees, switchbacking from orchard to orchard, riding along the rim of the sky in a tremendous serration of rebounding dives and ascensions. Suddenly it ended. He mounted like a rocket, curved over in splendid parabola, dived down through cumulus of pigeons. One bird fell back, gashed dead, looking astonished, like a man falling out of a tree. The ground came up and crushed it.

J A Baker

Monet Refuses the Operation

Doctor, you say there are no haloes
around the streetlights in Paris
and what I see is an aberration
caused by old age, an affliction.
I tell you it has taken me all my life
to arrive at the vision of gas lamps as angels,
to soften and blur and finally banish
the edges you regret I don't see,
to learn that the line I called the horizon
does not exist and sky and water,
so long apart, are the same state of being.
Fifty-four years before I could see
Rouen cathedral is built
of parallel shafts of sun,
and now you want to restore
my youthful errors: fixed
notions of top and bottom,
the illusion of three-dimensional space,
wisteria separate
from the bridge it covers.
What can I say to convince you
the Houses of Parliament dissolve
night after night to become
the fluid dream of the Thames?
I will not return to a universe
of objects that don't know each other,
as if islands were not the lost children
of one great continent. The world
is flux, and light becomes what it touches,
becomes water, lilies on water,
above and below water,
becomes lilac and mauve and yellow
and white and cerulean lamps,
small fists passing sunlight
so quickly to one another
that it would take long, streaming hair

inside my brush to catch it.
To paint the speed of light!
Our weighted shapes, these verticals,
burn to mix with air
and change our bones, skin, clothes
to gases. Doctor,
if only you could see
how heaven pulls earth into its arms
and how infinitely the heart expands
to claim this world, blue vapor without end.

Lisel Mueller

II : Living

There is no event so common-place but that God is present within it, always hidden, always leaving you room to recognize him or not to recognize him... If I were called upon to state in a few words the essence of everything I was trying to say both as a novelist and as a preacher, it would be something like this: Listen to your life. See it for the fathomless mystery that it is. In the boredom and pain of it no less than in the excitement and gladness: touch, taste, smell your way to the heavenly and hidden heart of it because in the last analysis all moments are key moments, and life itself is grace.

Frederick Buechner

At First, My Daughter

She is world without understanding.
She is made of sound.
She drinks me.

We laugh when I lift her by the feet.
She is new as a petal.
Water comes out of her mouth and her little crotch.

She gives the crook of my arm
A weight of delight.
I stare in her moving mirror of untouched flesh.

Absurd, but verifiable,
These words – mother, daughter –
They taste of receiving and relinquishing.

She will never again be quite so novel and lovely
Nor I so astonished.
In touch, we are celebrating

The first and last moments
Of being together and separate
Indissolute – till we are split

By time, and growth, and man,
The things I made her with.

Elma Mitchell

Soap Suds

This brand of soap has the same smell as once in the big
House he visited when he was eight: the walls of the bathroom open
To reveal a lawn where a great yellow ball rolls back through a hoop
To rest at the head of a mallet held in the hands of a child.

And these were the joys of that house: a tower with a telescope;
Two great faded globes, one of the earth, one of the stars;
A stuffed black dog in the hall; a walled garden with bees;
A rabbit warren; a rockery; a vine under glass; the sea.

To which he has now returned. The day of course is fine
And a grown-up voice cries Play! The mallet slowly swings,
Then crack, a great gong booms from the dog-dark hall and the ball
Skims forward through the hoop and then through the next and then

Through hoops where no hoops were and each dissolves in turn
And the grass has grown head-high and an angry voice cries Play!
But the ball is lost and the mallet slipped long since from the hands
Under the running tap that are not the hands of a child.

Louis MacNeice

The River Orb

She sings,
her small form squat in the canoe
on the green river
laughing as she tumbles through the rapids
climbing out to lead the boat through the shallows
sometimes freeing her slender purple form
from the rounded helmet and padded jacket
to swim in the cool clear pools
before once again grasping the yellow paddle
and resuming her sunny task.

Her twin, more intent
brow furrowed in concentration
paddles soreness into her hands
enjoying not the movement of the boat
but the electric blue of damselflies
the passing of an egret overhead
slipping into the water to swim with the fish
settling gradually to the task
arriving tired but victorious.

The boy
master of all he surveys
paddles now languid
now with muscles rippling through the water
returning upstream to investigate
finally disappearing downriver with a shrug.
We find him motionless
a single form with his kayak
mirrored in the still water of the landing stage
waiting, being, with the resignation of his years.

The father
reckons he's easily the worst on the river
furious with confusion
sets his jaw, teaches himself to relax
learns to go with the flow, backwards

down the rapids
losing paddle and barrel
allowing himself to be rescued by a stranger
kept cheerful by the singing child.
The hours pass
bowing to the flowing water
and he too arrives victorious.

And me. Perhaps it's true.
Perhaps most of my life is rapids
taken voluntarily
without always anticipating the pain
occasionally stranded, battling, discouraged
sometimes exhilarated, adventurous
learning just to keep going
to enjoy the pools of calm
to soak my hot body in the clear waters
listen to the happiness of the passing wagtail
to store it up, paint and share it
before moving on again
round the next bend.

Alison Morgan

May my heart always be open

may my heart always be open to little
birds who are the secrets of living
whatever they sing is better than to know
and if men should not hear them men are old

may my mind stroll about hungry
and fearless and thirsty and supple
and even if it's sunday may i be wrong
for whenever men are right they are not young

and may myself do nothing usefully
and love yourself so more than truly
there's never been quite such a fool who could fail
pulling all the sky over him with one smile

e e cummings

A Summer Morning

Her young employers, having got in late
From seeing friends in town
And scraped the right front fender on the gate,
Will not, the cook expects, be coming down.

She makes a quiet breakfast for herself.
The coffee-pot is bright,
The jelly where it should be on the shelf.
She breaks an egg into the morning light,

Then, with the bread-knife lifted, stands and hears
The sweet efficient sounds
Of thrush and catbird, and the snip of shears
Where, in the terraced backward of the grounds,

A gardener works before the heat of day.
He straightens for a view
Of the big house ascending stony-gray
Out of his beds mosaic with the dew.

His young employers having got in late,
He and the cook alone
Receive the morning on their old estate,
Possessing what the owners can but own.

Richard Wilbur

This is Just to Say

I have eaten
the plums
that were in
the icebox

and which
you were probably
saving
for breakfast

Forgive me
they were delicious
so sweet
and so cold

William Carlos Williams

So Much Happiness

It is difficult to know what to do with so much happiness.
With sadness there is something to rub against,
a wound to tend with lotion and cloth.
When the world falls in around you, you have pieces to pick up,
something to hold in your hands, like ticket stubs or change.

But happiness floats.
It doesn't need you to hold it down.
It doesn't need anything.
Happiness lands on the roof of the next house, singing,
and disappears when it wants to.
You are happy either way.
Even the fact that you once lived in a peaceful tree house
and now live over a quarry of noise and dust
cannot make you unhappy.
Everything has a life of its own,
it too could wake up filled with possibilities
of coffee cake and ripe peaches,
and love even the floor which needs to be swept,
the soiled linens and scratched records...

Since there is no place large enough
to contain so much happiness,
you shrug, you raise your hands, and it flows out of you
into everything you touch. You are not responsible.
You take no credit, as the night sky takes no credit
For the moon, but continues to hold it, and share it,
And in that way, be known.

Naomi Shihab Nye

At the Fishhouses

Although it is a cold evening,
down by one of the fishhouses
an old man sits netting,
his net, in the gloaming almost invisible,
a dark purple-brown,
and his shuttle worn and polished.
The air smells so strong of codfish
it makes one's nose run and one's eyes water.
The five fishhouses have steeply peaked roofs
and narrow, cleated gangplanks slant up
to storerooms in the gables
for the wheelbarrows to be pushed up and down on.
All is silver: the heavy surface of the sea,
swelling slowly as if considering spilling over,
is opaque, but the silver of the benches,
the lobster pots, and masts, scattered
among the wild jagged rocks,
is of an apparent translucence
like the small old buildings with an emerald moss
growing on their shoreward walls.
The big fish tubs are completely lined
with layers of beautiful herring scales
and the wheelbarrows are similarly plastered
with creamy iridescent coats of mail,
With small iridescent flies crawling on them.

Up on the little slope behind the houses,
set in the sparse bright sprinkle of grass,
is an ancient wooden capstan,
cracked, with two long bleached handles
and some melancholy stains, like dried blood,
where the ironwork has rusted.
The old man accepts a Lucky Strike.
He was a friend of my grandfather.
We talk of the decline in the population
and of codfish and herring

while he waits for a herring boat to come in.
There are sequins on his vest and on his thumb.
He has scraped the scales, the principal beauty,
from unnumbered fish with that black old knife,
the blade of which is almost worn away.

Down at the water's edge, at the place
where they haul up the boats, up the long ramp
descending into the water, thin silver
tree trunks are laid horizontally
across the gray stones, down and down
at intervals of four or five feet.

Cold dark deep and absolutely clear,
element bearable to no mortal,
to fish and to seals... One seal particularly
I have seen here evening after evening.
He was curious about me. He was interested in music;
like me a believer in total immersion,
so I used to sing him Baptist hymns.
I also sang 'A Mighty Fortress Is Our God'.
He stood up in the water and regarded me
steadily, moving his head a little.
Then he would disappear, then suddenly emerge
almost in the same spot, with a sort of shrug
as if it were against his better judgment.
Cold dark deep and absolutely clear,
the clear gray icy water... Back, behind us,
the dignified tall firs begin.
Bluish, associating with their shadows,
a million Christmas trees stand
waiting for Christmas. The water seems suspended
above the rounded gray and blue-gray stones.

I have seen it over and over, the same sea, the same,
slightly, indifferently swinging above the stones,
icily free above the stones,
above the stones and then the world.
If you should dip your hand in,

your wrist would ache immediately,
your bones would begin to ache and your hand would burn
as if the water were a transmutation of fire
that feeds on stones and burns with a dark gray flame.
If you tasted it, it would first taste bitter,
then briny, then surely burn your tongue.
It is like what we imagine knowledge to be:
dark, salt, clear, moving, utterly free,
drawn from the cold hard mouth
of the world, derived from the rocky breasts
forever, flowing and drawn, and since
our knowledge is historical, flowing, and flown.

Elizabeth Bishop

Cathedral Builders

They climbed on sketchy ladders towards God,
With winch and pulley hoisted hewn rock into heaven,
Inhabited sky with hammers, defied gravity,
Deified stone, took up God's house to meet Him,

And came down to their suppers and small beer;
Every night slept, lay with their smelly wives,
Quarrelled and cuffed the children, lied,
Spat, sang, were happy or unhappy,

And every day took to the ladders again;
Impeded the rights of way of another summer's
Swallows, grew greyer, shakier, became less inclined
To fix a neighbour's roof of a fine evening,

Saw naves sprout arches, clerestories soar,
Cursed the loud fancy glaziers for their luck,
Somehow escaped the plague, got rheumatism,
Decided it was time to give it up,

To leave the spire to others; stood in the crowd
Well back from the vestments at the consecration,
Envied the fat bishop his warm boots,
Cocked up a squint eye and said, "1 bloody did that".

John Ormerod

Stonemasons at work in the 14th century

Drystone

In sooty streams across the hill, rough, bumpy,
contoured in jagging falls and twists, they walk
beyond the crest, beyond the muddy clough,
children's coarse pencil sentences, deep-scored,
staggering across a thick absorbing sheet, dry frontiers
on a wet land, dry streams across wet earth,
coal-dry, soot-dry, carrying the wind's black leavings
from the mill valley, but against the gales
low, subtle, huddling; needs more than wind to scatter them.

There is no glue, there is no mortar subtle,
solid enough for here: only the stained air blowing
up from the brewery through the lean dry gaps;
hard to know how an eye once saw the consonance,
the fit of these unsocial shapes, once saw
each one pressed to the other's frontier, every one
inside the other's edge, and conjured the dry aliens
to run, one sentence scrawled across the sheet,
subtle against the wind, a silent spell, a plot.

Rowan Williams

The English Archer

Of the archer himself we shall learn much more, from a detail here or a clue there, as we go on. Broadly speaking he was drawn from the villages and fields, a man of small property, sometimes none, sometimes an outlaw or a poacher pardoned for service; a man of no great estimation in the world, but a man of country skills and strength, rough living and hard working, accustomed to things of wood and finding a pleasing familiarity in the wooden bow, and the competition and emulation of practice at the butts, which by the time of Edward III's reign were common to every small town and very many villages throughout the country.

He wore sometimes a steel cap, sometimes a querbole, or hardened leather helmet with an iron rim and crosspieces, a quilted jacket with iron plates sewn on the inside, or a mail shirt, more or less of a uniform according to the military fashions of the time and the attitudes of those who employed him, serviceable boots and hose, and had a sword at his side, a dagger, a maul, or some other weapon for hand-to-hand fighting.

On his back he carried all the necessities of his daily life, cloak for rain and sleeping, spare clothes if he could provide them, water bottle and food pack. With two quivers at his back, he shouldered his bow

Archers, Luttrell Psalter, 14th century

in its canvas bowcase and marched his way to much estimation in Britain, and after 1346 to find great esteem and to inspire great dread throughout Europe.

It had been hard to train him to his best; it proved impossible to keep him to it; but at his best there was no man in the world to beat him, no matter the odds against him; and his breed lasted long beyond the longbow; he used the musket and the rifle; he endured in 1915 the same, and worse, than his forefathers suffered in 1415.

There has been a fashion lately to deride, not his kind, but his service to his nation as an exploitation by his rulers of his servitude and simplicity. Neither he nor his nation has ever taken kindly to servitude, and often his simplicity turns out to have been a reticence, which once dropped when overt action has to be taken, is found by his enemies to have concealed both dogged and dashing courage, subtlety together with intransigence, and a total refusal to yield to pressures from outside his nation or from within it that are not acceptable to his not quickly formed but formidably defended attitudes. He will never entirely perish because, for all the sloth and the cantankerous emulation that lie side by side in his nature, he shares with the best of mankind, courage, clear sight and honesty.

Robert Hardy

What's Left

(for Peter Hennessy)

I used to wait for the flowers,
my pleasure reposed on them.
Now I like plants before they get to the blossom.
Leafy ones – foxgloves, comfrey, delphiniums –
fleshy tiers of strong leaves pushing up
into air grown daily lighter and more sheened
with bright dust like the eyeshadow
that tall young woman in the bookshop wears,
its shimmer and crumble on her white lids.

The washing sways on the line, the sparrows pull
at the heaps of drying weeds that I've left around.
Perhaps this is middle age. Untidy, unfinished,
knowing there'll never be time now to finish,
liking the plants – their strong lives –
not caring about flowers, sitting in weeds
to write things down, look at things,
watching the sway of shirts on the line,
the cloth filtering light.

I know more or less
how to live through my life now.
But I want to know how to live what's left
with my eyes open and my hands open;
I want to stand at the door in the rain
listening, sniffing, gaping.
Fearful and joyous,
like an idiot before God.

Kerry Hardie

He Retraced his Steps

He retraced his steps back
to the point of decision
and failure, and scanned the
horizon for a new route.

It is not an exact science,
and the knowledge he carried
was a heavy weight. There,
in a gap between the trees,

was the path he took before.
Its obvious unsuitability
mocked him. And seeing
how one thing led to

another, he stared down
the Roman Road straightness
of all the things that
hindsight could correct.

Enough. There were reasons
as well as excuses. Pushing
aside the branches, he strode
again the path he knew was his.

Stephen Cottrell

The Pilgrim

Who would true Valour see,
Let him come hither;
One here will constant be,
Come Wind, come Weather.
There's no *Discouragement*,
Shall make him once *Relent*,
His first avowed *Intent*,
To be a Pilgrim.

Whoso beset him round
With dismal *Stories*
Do but themselves confound;
His Strength the *more* is.
No *Lion* can him fright,
He'll with a *Giant* fight,
But he will have a right
To be a Pilgrim.

Hobgoblin nor foul *Fiend*
Can *daunt* his Spirit,
He knows he *at the end*
Shall Life Inherit.
Then Fancies fly away,
He'll fear not what men say,
He'll labour Night and Day
To be a Pilgrim.

John Bunyan

Pilgrim's Progress (1684)

Road

Traveller, your footprints are
the only path, the only track
wayfarer, there is no way,
there is no map or Northern star,
just a blank page and a starless dark;
and should you turn round to admire
the distance that you've made today
the road will billow into dust.
No way on and no way back,
there is no way, my comrade: trust
your own quick step, the end's delay,
the vanished trail of your own wake,
wayfarer, sea-walker, Christ.

Don Paterson

The Place Where We Are Right

From the place where we are right
Flowers will never grow
In the spring.

The place where we are right
Is hard and trampled
Like a yard.

But doubts and loves
Dig up the world
Like a mole, a plow.
And a whisper will be heard in the place
Where the ruined
House once stood.

Yehuda Amichai

Lying in a Hammock at William Duffy's Farm in Pine Island, Minnesota

Over my head, I see the bronze butterfly,
Asleep on the black trunk,
Blowing like a leaf in green shadow.
Down the ravine behind the empty house,
The cowbells follow one another
Into the distances of the afternoon.
To my right,
In a field of sunlight between two pines,
The droppings of last year's horses
Blaze up into golden stones.
I lean back, as the evening darkens and comes on.
A chicken hawk floats over, looking for home.
I have wasted my life.

James Wright

The Guest House

This human being is a guesthouse.
Every morning a new arrival.

A joy, a depression, a meanness,
some momentary awareness comes
as an unexpected visitor.

Welcome and entertain them all!
Even if they're a crowd of sorrows,
who violently sweep your house
empty of its furniture,
still, treat each guest honorably.
He may be clearing you out
for some new delight.

The dark thought, the shame, the malice,
meet them at the door laughing,
and invite them in.

Be grateful for whoever comes,
because each has been sent
as a guide from beyond.

Jalal ad-Din Muhammad Rumi

Translated from the Persian by
Coleman Barks with John Moyne

The Quarrel

Suddenly, after the quarrel, while we waited,
Disheartened, silent, with downcast looks, nor stirred
Eyelid nor finger, hopeless both, yet hoping
Against all hope to unsay the sundering word:

While all the room's stillness deepened, deepened about us
And each of us crept his thought's way to discover
How, with as little sound as the fall of a leaf,
The shadow had fallen, and lover quarreled with lover;

And while, in the quiet, I marveled – alas, alas –
At your deep beauty, your tragic beauty, torn
As the pale flower is torn by the wanton sparrow –
This beauty, pitied and loved, and now forsworn;

It was then, when the instant darkened to its darkest, –
When faith was lost with hope, and the rain conspired
To strike its gray arpeggios against our heartstrings, –
When love no longer dared, and scarcely desired:

It was then that suddenly, in the neighbor's room,
The music started: that brave quartette of strings
Breaking out of the stillness, as out of our stillness,
Like the indomitable heart of life that sings

When all is lost; and startled from our sorrow,
Tranced from our grief by that diviner grief,
We raised remembering eyes, each looked at other,
Blinded with tears of joy; and another leaf

Fell silently as that first; and in the instant
The shadow had gone, our quarrel became absurd;
And we rose, to the angelic voices of the music,
And I touched your hand, and we kissed, without a word.

Conrad Aiken

Music

One of the most important facts about music is that it is a thing to be *understood*, and understanding music is not a matter of exploring neural pathways or acoustical relations, but a matter of attending to and grasping the intrinsic order and meaning of events in musical space. Furthermore music is an *appearance*. If you look for music in the order of nature, you will not find it. Of course, you will find sounds, which is to say pitched vibrations, caused as a rule by human activity, and impinging on the ears of those who listen to them. But you won't find any of the features that distinguish music. For example, you won't find the space in which music moves. You won't find the gravitational forces that bring melodies to rest or make the notes of a chord cohere as a single entity. You won't find melodies – those strange things that begin and end and move through musical space between their vivid edges. You won't find tones – the elements from which melodies are composed – but only the pitched sounds in which we hear them. Music is all appearance, and yet it is not an illusion or a passing veneer that we could fail to notice and be none the worse for not noticing. It is out there and not in here, to use the familiar metaphors – though note that they are metaphors, which might be both illuminating and misleading when it comes to spelling them out.

Roger Scruton

I remember a morning about fifteen years ago. It was a particularly bad morning, after a particularly bad night. We had been caught in

one of those cyclical rows that reignite every time you think they've come to an exhausted close, because the thing that's wrong won't be left alone, won't stay out of sight if you try to turn away from it. ... When daylight came, the whole world seemed worn out. We got up, and she went to work. I went to a cafe and nursed my misery along with a cappuccino. I could not see any way out of sorrow that did not involve some obvious self-deception, some wishful lie about where we'd got to. ... And then the person serving in the cafe put on a cassette: Mozart's Clarinet Concerto, the middle movement, the Adagio.

If you don't know it, it is a very patient piece of music. It too goes round and round, in its way, essentially playing the same tune again and again, on the clarinet alone and then with the orchestra, clarinet and then orchestra, lifting up the same unhurried lilt of solitary sound, and then backing it with a kind of messageless tenderness in deep waves, when the strings join in. It is not strained in any way. It does not sound as if Mozart is doing something he can only just manage, and it does not sound as if the music is struggling to lift a weight it can only just manage. Yet at the same time, it is not music that denies anything. It offers a strong, absolutely calm rejoicing, but it does not pretend there is no sorrow. On the contrary, it sounds as if it comes from a world where sorrow is perfectly ordinary but still there is more to be said. I had heard it lots of times, but this time it felt to me like news. It said: everything you fear is true. And yet. And yet. Everything you have done wrong, you have really done wrong. And yet. And yet. The world is wider than you fear it is, wider than the repeating rigmaroles in your mind, and it has this in it, as truly as it contains your unhappiness. Shut up and listen, and let yourself count, just a little bit, on a calm that you do not have to be able to make for yourself, because here it is, freely offered. You are still deceiving yourself, said the music, if you don't allow for the possibility of *this*. There is more going on here than what you deserve, or don't deserve. There is *this*, as well. And it played the tune again, with all the cares in the world.

The novelist Richard Powers has written that the Clarinet Concerto sounds the way mercy would sound, and that's exactly how I experienced it.

Francis Spufford

Nursing a Grudge

Initially her
grudge was
so small
she weaned
it on
the breast.
As it
grew,
she nursed
it lovingly:
feeding,
cleaning,
always
monitoring vital-signs.

One day, her
grudge
nearly died,
but she
refused
to let go,
massaging it back to life.

The more
she gave her
precious grudge,
the more
it took,
becoming:
big,
strong,
healthy,
until it wouldn't let her go.

They say
it was
the patient
she nursed
so well that eventually
throttled her.

Tim Sumpter

Otherwise

I got out of bed
on two strong legs.
It might have been
otherwise. I ate
cereal, sweet
milk, ripe, flawless
peach. It might
have been otherwise.
I took the dog uphill
to the birchwood.
All morning I did
the work I love.

At noon I lay down
with my mate. It might
have been otherwise.
We ate dinner together
at a table with silver
candlesticks. It might
have been otherwise.
I slept in a bed
in a room with paintings
on the walls, and
planned another day
just like this day.
But one day, I know,
it will be otherwise.

Jane Kenyon

Ithaca

You're ready now to sail for Ithaca?
Then make a wish your journey be a long one,
Filled with adventures, with discoveries.
As for the Laistrygonians, the Cyclops,
The fury of Poseidon – don't be afraid of these.
You won't meet anything like them, provided that
Your thoughts aim high, while delicate, ethereal
Emotions seize your body and your spirit.
The Laistrygonians and the Cyclops, or
Savage Poseidon won't appear, unless
You bring them with you in your soul, unless
Your soul unleash them to confront you.

Yes... May your journey be a long one.
May there be many summer mornings
When – with what enchantment and what joy! –
You'll land in harbours never seen before,
To linger by a merchant's wares from Sidon,
And bargain with him for his gems and finery
(Mother of pearl and corals, amber and ebony);
And purchase in abundance perfumes of every kind,
Intoxicating perfumes, sensual – all you can.
And may you come to many towns in Egypt,
To learn, and go on learning, from the wise.

Always keep Ithaca steadily in mind:
Your voyage is not over till you step ashore.
But let there be no sense of urgency.
Far better that your journey last for many years,
Better to reach the island as an older man,
Enriched by all the treasures you've acquired,
And not expecting any gifts from Ithaca.

Ithaca gave you this voyage of delights:
Except for her, you'd never have set sail.
But she has nothing left to give you now.

Ithaca won't have cheated you, although you find her poor.
You'll be a wiser man by then, have seen it all,
And understand what all these Ithacas may mean.

Constantine Cavafy

Translated by Patrick Boyde

Odysseus departs from the land of the Phaeacians
Detail from Claude Lorrain (1646)

III. Loving

There is only one starting place: discovering what it means to be loved. For most of us, by parents; for the fortunate, by friends, husband, wife or partner; for all of us by God. I have spent my life betting that there is a cause, an origin, of everything that exists, that (despite the darkness) there is a reason for beauty, compassion and goodness, and that to name the source from which they constantly spring, to name the true ground of love and to define it, is to name God.

Michael Mayne

if i have made...

if i have made,my lady,intricate
imperfect various things chiefly which wrong
your eyes(frailer than most deep dreams are frail)
songs less firm than your body's whitest song
upon my mind – if i have failed to snare
the glance too shy – if through my singing slips
the very skillful strangeness of your smile
the keen primeval silence of your hair

– let the world say "his most wise music stole
nothing from death" –
                        you only will create
(who are so perfectly alive)my shame:
lady through whose profound and fragile lips
the sweet small clumsy feet of April came

into the ragged meadow of my soul.

e e cummings

Love Without Hope

Love without hope, as when the young bird-catcher
Swept off his tall hat to the Squire's own daughter,
So let the imprisoned larks escape and fly
Singing about her head, as she rode by.

Ecstasy of Chaos

When the immense drugged universe explodes
In a cascade of unendurable colour
And leaves us gasping naked,
This is no more than the ecstasy of chaos:
Hold fast, with both hands, to that royal love
Which alone, as we know certainly, restores
Fragmentation into true being.

She Tells Her Love While Half Asleep

She tells her love while half asleep,
    In the dark hours,
        With half-words whispered low:
As Earth stirs in her winter sleep
    And puts out grass and flowers
        Despite the snow,
        Despite the falling snow.

Robert Graves

What Love Does

This is what love does. This is what you say:
'Behold I love you in all languages, in all hearts and in all stars.
I am spread skyward to mate with the moon, swarm with the sea,
Convulse with the fire of the sun.
Behold, I walk unharmed in the flames of joy
And even the clang of silence stays unheard.
Behold, I talk with God to God's face
And fly with angels in a further sky.'
Enjoy it as long as you can. You'll remember it fondly,
This flying with angels, this chatting with God on equal terms.

Louis de Bernières

Song of Songs

I am a rose of Sharon,
   a lily of the valleys.
As a lily among brambles,
   so is my love among maidens.
As an apple tree among the trees of the wood,
   so is my beloved among young men.
With great delight I sat in his shadow,
   and his fruit was sweet to my taste.
He brought me to the banqueting house,
   and his intention towards me was love.
Sustain me with raisins,
   refresh me with apples;
   for I am faint with love.

      How beautiful you are, my love,
         how very beautiful!
      Your eyes are doves
         behind your veil.
      Your hair is like a flock of goats,
         moving down the slopes of Gilead.
      Your teeth are like a flock of shorn ewes
         that have come up from the washing,
      all of which bear twins,
         and not one among them is bereaved.
      Your lips are like a crimson thread,
         and your mouth is lovely.
      Your cheeks are like halves of a pomegranate
         behind your veil.
      Your two breasts are like two fawns,
         twins of a gazelle,
         that feed among the lilies.
      Until the day breathes
         and the shadows flee,
      I will hasten to the mountain of myrrh
         and the hill of frankincense.
      You are altogether beautiful, my love;
         there is no flaw in you.

Awake, O north wind,
  and come, O south wind!
Blow upon my garden
  that its fragrance may be wafted abroad.
Let my beloved come to his garden,
  and eat its choicest fruits.
My beloved is all radiant and ruddy,
  distinguished among ten thousand.
His head is the finest gold;
  his locks are wavy,
  black as a raven.
His eyes are like doves
  beside springs of water,
bathed in milk,
  fitly set.
His cheeks are like beds of spices,
  yielding fragrance.
His lips are lilies,
  distilling liquid myrrh.
His arms are rounded gold,
  set with jewels.
His body is ivory work,
  encrusted with sapphires.
His legs are alabaster columns,
  set upon bases of gold.
His appearance is like Lebanon,
  choice as the cedars.
His speech is most sweet,
  and he is altogether desirable.
This is my beloved and this is my friend,
  O daughters of Jerusalem.

Many waters cannot quench love,
  neither can floods drown it.

from *The Song of Solomon*

Home From Abroad

Far-fetched with tales of other worlds and ways,
My skin well-oiled with wines of the Levant,
I set my face into a filial smile
To greet the pale, domestic kiss of Kent.

But shall I never learn? That gawky girl,
Recalled so primly in my foreign thoughts,
Becomes again the green-haired queen of love
Whose wanton form dilates as it delights.

Her rolling tidal landscape floods the eye
And drowns Chianti in a dusky stream;
he flower-flecked grasses swim with simple horses,
The hedges choke with roses fat as cream.

So do I breathe the hayblown airs of home,
And watch the sea-green elms drip birds and shadows,
And as the twilight nets the plunging sun
My heart's keel slides to rest among the meadows.

Laurie Lee

Judging Distances

Not only how far away, but the way that you say it
Is very important. Perhaps you may never get
The knack of judging a distance, but at least you know
How to report on a landscape: the central sector,
The right of the arc and that, which we had last Tuesday,
        And at least you know

That maps are of time, not place, so far as the army
Happens to be concerned – the reason being,
Is one which need not delay us. Again, you know
There are three kinds of tree, three only, the fir and the poplar,
And those which have bushy tops to; and lastly
        That things only seem to be things.

A barn is not called a barn, to put it more plainly,
Or a field in the distance, where sheep may be safely grazing.
You must never be over-sure. You must say, when reporting:
At five o'clock in the central sector is a dozen
Of what appear to be animals; whatever you do,
        Don't call the bleeders sheep.

I am sure that's quite clear; and suppose, for the sake of example,
The one at the end, asleep, endeavours to tell us
What he sees over there to the west, and how far away,
After first having come to attention. There to the west,
On the fields of summer the sun and the shadows bestow
        Vestments of purple and gold.

The still white dwellings are like a mirage in the heat,
And under the swaying elms a man and a woman
Lie gently together. Which is, perhaps, only to say
That there is a row of houses to the left of the arc,
And that under some poplars a pair of what appear to be humans
        Appear to be loving.

Well that, for an answer, is what we rightly call
Moderately satisfactory only, the reason being,

Is that two things have been omitted, and those are very important.
The human beings, now: in what direction are they,
And how far away, would you say? And do not forget
        There may be dead ground in between.

There may be dead ground in between; and I may not have got
The knack of judging a distance; I will only venture
A guess that perhaps between me and the apparent lovers,
(Who, incidentally, appear by now to have finished,)
At seven o'clock from the houses, is roughly a distance
        Of about one year and a half.

Henry Reed

Poplars in the sun
Claude Monet (1887)

Sonnet 116

Let me not to the marriage of true minds
Admit impediments. Love is not love
Which alters when it alteration finds,
Or bends with the remover to remove:
O no; it is an ever-fixed mark,
That looks on tempests, and is never shaken;
It is the star to every wandering bark,
Whose worth's unknown, although his height be taken.
Love's not Time's fool, though rosy lips and cheeks
Within his bending sickle's compass come;
Love alters not with his brief hours and weeks,
But bears it out even to the edge of doom.
   If this be error and upon me proved,
   I never writ, nor no man ever loved.

Sonnet 29

When, in disgrace with fortune and men's eyes,
I all alone beweep my outcast state,
And trouble deaf heaven with my bootless cries,
And look upon myself, and curse my fate,
Wishing me like to one more rich in hope,
Featur'd like him, like him with friends possess'd,
Desiring this man's art and that man's scope,
With what I most enjoy contented least;
Yet in these thoughts myself almost despising,
Haply I think on thee, and then my state,
Like to the lark at break of day arising
From sullen earth, sings hymns at heaven's gate;
For thy sweet love remember'd such wealth brings
That then I scorn to change my state with kings.

William Shakespeare

He Loved...

He loved three things alone:
Evensong, white peacocks
And old maps of America.
He hated it when children cried,
He hated tea with raspberry jam
And women's hysterics.
... And he had married me.

Anna Akhmatova

Translated by D M Thomas

Alone

Nothing will fill the salt caves our youth wore:
Happiness later nor a house with corn
Ripe to its walls and open door.
We filtered through to sky and flowed into
A pit full of stars; so we are each alone.
Even in this being alone I meet with you.

E J Scovell

Climbing My Grandfather

I decide to do it free, without a rope or net.
First, the old brogues, dusty and cracked;
an easy scramble onto his trousers,
pushing into the weave, trying to get a grip.
By the overhanging shirt I change
direction, traverse along his belt
to an earth-stained hand. The nails
are splintered and give good purchase,
the skin of his finger is smooth and thick
like warm ice. On his arm I discover
the glassy ridge of a scar, place my feet
gently in the old stitches and move on.
At his still firm shoulder, I rest for a while
in the shade, not looking down,
for climbing has its dangers, then pull
myself up the loose skin of his neck
to a smiling mouth to drink among teeth.
Refreshed, I cross the screed cheek,
to stare into his brown eyes, watch a pupil
slowly open and close. Then up over
the forehead, the wrinkles well-spaced
and easy, to his thick hair (soft and white
at this altitude), reaching for the summit,
where gasping for breath I can only lie
watching clouds and birds circle,
feeling his heat, knowing
the slow pulse of his good heart.

Andrew Waterhouse

Bone of my Bone

Thirteen years.
Your soft child's body begins to strengthen
look not like warm flesh on bendable bone
but taut muscles stretched over a frame.
You begin to assume independence
shoulder responsibility
and your gaze meets mine
steady, still loving
remembering the warmth of the arms that held you
but now smiling as an equal
as you mend my bicycle chain.
A phase is ending, another beginning;
will you remember, through the storms that lie ahead
that it was I who made you
bonded with you, fed you, played with you
gave you the seeds of manhood
growing now within you?
Your growth will change me too
for as dependence dies
new relationship is born.
May I know how to let you grow
into your brave new world.

Alison Morgan

A Valediction : Forbidding Mourning

As virtuous men pass mildly away,
  And whisper to their souls, to go,
Whilst some of their sad friends do say,
  The breath goes now, and some say, no:

So let us melt, and make no noise,
  No tear-floods, nor sigh-tempests move,
'Twere profanation of our joys
  To tell the laity our love.

Moving of th'earth brings harms and fears,
  Men reckon what it did and meant,
But trepidation of the spheares,
  Though greater far, is innocent.

Dull sublunary lovers' love
  (Whose soul is sense) cannot admit
Absence, because it doth remove
  Those things which elemented it.

But we by a love, so much refin'd
  That our selves know not what it is,
Inter-assured of the mind,
  Care less, eyes, lips, and hands to miss.

Our two souls therefore, which are one,
  Though I must goe, endure not yet
A breach, but an expansion,
  Like gold to aery thinness beat.

If they be two, they are two so
  As stiff twin compasses are two,
Thy soule the fixed foot, makes no show
  To move, but doth, if th'other do.

And though it in the centre sit,
  Yet when the other far doth roam,
It leans, and hearkens after it,

And grows erect, as that comes home.

Such wilt thou be to me, who must
  Like th'other foot, obliquely run;
Thy firmness makes my circle just,
  And makes me end, where I begun.

John Donne

Measuring with a compass
from a 14th century manuscript of Euclid's *Elements*

We Sat at the Window

Bournemouth, 1875

We sat at the window looking out,
And the rain came down like silken strings
That Swithin's day. Each gutter and spout
Babbled unchecked in the busy way
      Of witless things:
Nothing to read, nothing to see
Seemed in that room for her and me
      On Swithin's day.

We were irked by the scene, by our own selves; yes,
For I did not know, nor did she infer
How much there was to read and guess
By her in me, and to see and crown
      By me in her.
Wasted were two souls in their prime,
And great was the waste, that July time
      When the rain came down.

Thomas Hardy

Rain, by Vincent Van Gogh

Sullen Moods

Love, never count your labour lost
Though I turn sullen or retired
Even at your side; my thought is crossed
With fancies by no evil fired.

And when I answer you, some days
Vaguely and wildly, never fear
That my love walks forbidden ways,
Snapping the ties that hold it here.

If I speak gruffly, this mood is
Mere indignation at my own
Shortcomings, plagues, uncertainties:
I forget the gentler tone.

You, now that you have come to be
My one beginning, prime and end,
I count at last as wholly me,
Lover no longer nor yet friend.

Help me to see you as before
When overwhelmed and dead, almost,
I stumbled on your secret door
Which saves the live man from the ghost.

Be once again the distant light,
Promise of glory, not yet known
 In full perfection – wasted quite
When on my imperfection thrown.

Robert Graves

The Arrow and the Song

I shot an arrow into the air,
It fell to earth, I knew not where;
For, so swiftly it flew, the sight
Could not follow it in its flight.

I breathed a song into the air,
It fell to earth, I knew not where;
For who has sight so keen and strong,
That it can follow the flight of song?

Long, long afterward, in an oak
I found the arrow, still unbroke;
And the song, from beginning to end,
I found again in the heart of a friend.

Henry Wadsworth Longfellow

Love and friendship

Love is like the wild rose-briar,
Friendship like the holly-tree –
The holly is dark when the rose-briar blooms
But which will bloom most constantly?

The wild-rose briar is sweet in the spring,
Its summer blossoms scent the air;
Yet wait till winter comes again
And who will call the wild-briar fair?

Then scorn the silly rose-wreath now
And deck thee with the holly's sheen,
That when December blights thy brow
He may still leave thy garland green.

Emily Jane Brontë

As well as the Bible and Shakespeare... ?

You are what   I would choose
for companion in the desert.
You would know the way out,
think providently about water.

in the solicitor's office.
You would have generous answers
for disagreeable contingencies.

on the motorway.
In your presence
I shouldn't notice tailbacks.

at the picnic.
You would have remembered matches,
have brought a surprise for the greedy.

at the funeral.
You would sneak gently with mourners,
But your hands would be warm with life.

U A Fanthorpe

The Man Who Travelled The World

He travelled the world, restless as rain.
There was no continent unexplored,
Scarcely a city unworthy of days, a night, a week.
In all these places he searched for her face
In the streets, in the parks, in the lanes,
Always pausing to look, listening out
For the voice he'd never heard yet, yet
Always knew he would know.

So many lovers, so many encounters,
So many years, so many lands.

Now he sits by the window, a cat in his lap,
An ancient man far from the place of his birth.
And inside that loosening frame of bones
Beats the same heart as the heart that
Beat in the young boy who knew she was there,
And set off to travel the world.

He thinks of the children he never had,
The ordinary things foregone,
The perverseness of such an exhausting,
Such an impossible search;
A whole life squandered on dreams.

It begins to rain. He puts on his glasses,
Looks through the window, watches the girls
Step by, avoiding the puddles, protecting
Their hair with their magazines.
He fondles the ears of the cat,
This ancient man far from the place of his birth,
Still looking, still in fief to the same unsatisfied heart
As the heart that beat in the young boy
Who knew she was there and
Set off to travel the world.

Louis de Bernières

A Marriage

We met
        under a shower
of bird-notes.
        Fifty years passed,
love's moment
        in a world in
servitude to time.
        She was young;
I kissed with my eyes
        closed and opened
them on her wrinkles.
        "Come," said death,
choosing her as his
        partner for
the last dance, And she,
        who in life
had done everything
        with a bird's grace,
opened her bill now
        for the shedding
of one sigh no
        heavier than a feather.

R S Thomas

À Quoi Bon Dire

Seventeen years ago you said
Something that sounded like Good-bye;
And everybody thinks that you are dead,
But I.

So I, as I grow stiff and cold
To this and that say Good-bye too;
And everybody sees that I am old
But you.

And one fine morning in a sunny lane
Some boy and girl will meet and kiss and swear
That nobody can love their way again
While over there
You will have smiled, I shall have tossed your hair.

Charlotte Mew

To Alexander Graham

Lying asleep walking
Last night I met my father
Who seemed pleased to see me.
He wanted to speak. I saw
His mouth saying something
But the dream had no sound.

We were surrounded by
Laid-up paddle steamers
In The Old Quay in Greenock.
I smelt the tar and the ropes.

It seemed that I was standing
Beside the big iron cannon
The tugs used to tie up to
When I was a boy. I turned
To see Dad standing just
Across the causeway under
That one lamp they keep on.

He recognised me immediately.
I could see that. He was
The handsome, same age
With his good brows as when
He would take me on Sundays
Saying we'll go for a walk.

Dad, what am I doing here?
What is it I am doing now?
Are you proud of me?
Going away, I knew
You wanted to tell me something.

You stopped and almost turned back
To say something. My father,
I try to be the best
In you you give me always.

Lying asleep turning
Round in the quay-lit dark
It was my father standing
As real as life. I smelt
The quay's tar and the ropes.

I think he wanted to speak.
But the dream had no sound.
I think I must have loved him.

W S Graham

IV. Trusting

Most people need poetry, but not much of it: it is a vitamin of which small familiar doses are enough. The poems most people know and enjoy and turn over and over again through their lives are like prayers addressed to the mystery of themselves.

Geoffrey Grigson

Prayer

Prayer the Church's banquet, angels' age,
    God's breath in man returning to his birth,
    The soul in paraphrase, heart in pilgrimage,
The Christian plummet sounding heav'n and earth
Engine against th' Almighty, sinners' tower,
    Reversèd thunder, Christ-side-piercing spear,
    The six-days' world transposing in an hour,
A kind of tune, which all things hear and fear;
Softness, and peace, and joy, and love, and bliss,
    Exalted manna, gladness of the best,
    Heaven in ordinary, man well dressed,
The milky way, the bird of Paradise,
    Church-bells beyond the stars heard, the soul's blood,
    The land of spices; something understood.

George Herbert

Saint Francis and The Birds

When Francis preached love to the birds
They listened, fluttered, throttled up
Into the blue like a flock of words

Released for fun from his holy lips.
Then wheeled back, whirred about his head,
Pirouetted on brothers' capes.

Danced on the wing, for sheer joy played
And sang, like images took flight.
Which was the best poem Francis made,

His argument true, his tone light.

Seamus Heaney

Psalm 121 : A Song of Ascents

I lift up my eyes to the hills.
   From where does my help come?
My help comes from the Lord,
   who made heaven and earth.
He will not let your foot be moved;
   he who keeps you will not slumber.
Behold, he who keeps Israel
   will neither slumber nor sleep.
The Lord is your keeper;
   the Lord is your shade on your right hand.
The sun shall not strike you by day,
   nor the moon by night.
The Lord will keep you from all evil;
   he will keep your life.
The Lord will keep
   your going out and your coming in
   from this time forth and for evermore.

God the Eater

There is a god in whom I do not believe
Yet to this god my love stretches,
This god whom I do not believe in is
My whole life, my life and I am his.

Everything that I have of pleasure and pain
(Of pain, of bitter pain and men's contempt)
I give this god for him to feed upon
As he is my whole life and I am his.

When I am dead I hope that he will eat
Everything I have been and have not been
And crunch and feed upon it and grow fat
Eating my life all up as it is his.

Stevie Smith

Yours, Not Ours

You are as inevitable as morning
and you are there
long before the first Woodbine croak is heard
at the bleary eyed bus stops of the city.
You watch and wonder
as the sound of waking
mumbles its chorus across roof tops
You see and hear lovers readjust their dreams
in the not quite right of day
You listen to the out of tune clatter of newspapers
drowning out the concert pitch spot-on of the trees
This is a tired morning, as street sweepers clock on
We have stolen it from you
and fashioned it in our own image
You have not yet charged us with theft
and when you do
our defence will be inadequate
the dog ends in the gutter have no apologies written on them
there are no acknowledgements in the personal columns
the milk bottles hold no thank you notes
and the morning yawns steadily onwards
the morning that is not ours
but always yours.

Stewart Henderson

Agnosticism

It doesn't come easy.

In spite of it all,
I can't help pushing open
the doors of country churches;
shoving a coin or two
in the box on the wall,
paying twice over
for the leaflet I take.

It doesn't come easy.

Wandering among gravestones
is irresistible;
departure is almost
impossible. I delay
it over and over
to hear once more the song of the blackbird.

It doesn't come easy.

As I race back
into the modern
rationalistic world,
I think of cathedral towns
and country rectories
and gentle rectors' wives
arranging the flowers.

John Tatum

Oil of Spikenard

What a spendthrift you are, sir,
A squander-seed wastrel!
Did they never teach you
The Puritan virtues?
Look at those puffball heads.
You toss your hair like a petulant schoolgirl, and there –
How untidy you are! – it's like dandruff.
Then there's sperm, not to mention the sand and the stars and the
                                            orange pips.
It's embarrassing, all this extravagance.

And not five minutes ago you painted a skyscape
In a whole fruit salad of pastels,
A study in citrus shades.
So now what are you up to?
You've rubbed it out and started again with blue.
Stop a minute and give us viewing time,
You throwaway artist.
Even when invention funds
are unlimited, surely the waste...

Couldn't this oil of spikenard
have been sold and given to the poor?

Anne Ashworth

The Virgin Punishing the Infant

He spoke early. Not the goo goo goo of infancy,
but I am God. Joseph kept away, carving himself
a silent Pinocchio out in the workshed. He said
he was a simple man and hadn't dreamed of this.

She grew anxious in that second year, would stare
at stars saying Gabriel, Gabriel. Your guess.
The village gossiped in the sun. The child was solitary,
his wide and solemn eyes could fill your head.

After he walked, our normal children crawled. Our wives
were first resentful, then superior. Mary's child
would bring her sorrow ... better far to have a son
who gurgled nonsense at your breast. Googoo. Googoo.

But I am God. We heard him through the window,
heard the smacks which made us peep. What we saw
was commonplace enough. But afterwards, we wondered
why the infant did not cry, why the Mother did.

Carol Ann Duffy

from Max Ernst, 'The Blessed Virgin
chastises the infant Jesus before three
witnesses' (1926)

At Communion

Whether I kneel or stand or sit in prayer
I am not caught in time nor held in space,
But, thrust beyond this posture, I am where
Time and eternity are face to face;
Infinity and space meet in this place
Where crossbar and upright hold the One
In agony and in all Love's embrace.
The power in helplessness which was begun
When all the brilliance of the flaming sun
Contained itself in the small confines of a child
Now comes to me in this strange action done
In mystery. Break time, break space, O wild
and lovely power. Break me: thus I am dead,
Am resurrected now in wine and bread.

Madeleine L'Engle

A Song of Joy

Sing aloud, O daughter Zion;
    shout, O Israel!
Rejoice and exult with all your heart,
    O daughter Jerusalem!
The Lord has taken away the judgments against you,
    he has turned away your enemies.
The king of Israel, the Lord, is in your midst;
    you shall fear disaster no more.

On that day it shall be said to Jerusalem:
Do not fear, O Zion;
    do not let your hands grow weak.
The Lord, your God, is in your midst,
    a warrior who gives victory;
he will rejoice over you with gladness,
    he will renew you in his love;
he will exult over you with loud singing
    as on a day of festival.

I will remove disaster from you,
    so that you will not bear reproach for it.
I will deal with all your oppressors
    at that time.
And I will save the lame
    and gather the outcast,
and I will change their shame into praise
    and renown in all the earth.

At that time I will bring you home,
    at the time when I gather you;
for I will make you renowned and praised
    among all the peoples of the earth,
when I restore your fortunes
    before your eyes, says the Lord.

The Prophet Zephaniah

You Held Me

You offered me a broken piece of bread.
I said I wanted jam and toast instead;
I said that bread was useless, basic, poor.
You offered me the bread and nothing more.

You stooped to wash the tiredness from my feet.
I said I need a bath to be complete;
And not from you so menial a chore.
You stooped to wash my feet and nothing more.

You overthrew the tables in my heart.
I said I like them as they are, apart;
I said it politely, showing you the door.
You overturned my heart and nothing more.

You held me like an etching in a press,
You held me, held me, held me, nothing less.

Stephen Cottrell

Jesus washing the disciples' feet, from a 14th century ivory

The Lake Isle of Innisfree

I will arise and go now, and go to Innisfree,
And a small cabin build there, of clay and wattles made:
Nine bean-rows will I have there, a hive for the honey-bee;
And live alone in the bee-loud glade.

And I shall have some peace there, for peace comes dropping slow,
Dropping from the veils of the morning to where the cricket sings;
There midnight's all a glimmer, and noon a purple glow,
And evening full of the linnet's wings.

I will arise and go now, for always night and day
I hear lake water lapping with low sounds by the shore;
While I stand on the roadway, or on the pavements grey,
I hear it in the deep heart's core.

W B Yeats

So Snugly I fit into Silence

So snugly I fit into silence
as the calmed bird in its high nest,

the baby in the round womb.
Here at last in my wordlessness you meet me.

Today I spoke in complaint of your smallness,
the narrow gaps between trees I saw you through;

tonight you tipped my gaze higher
and showed me again the stars,

the great bright wombs of them,
the great bright silence by which they praise you.

So fit I shining into silence snugly.
Tomorrow, I shall be born again.

Katy Morgan

Mission Impossible

He had been in paradise
Surrounded by a whole flotilla of angels
Each reflecting like mirrors
The warmth of the father;
We'll talk of this later. Well done,
My son. Stand back, to the angels
Their hot wings pressing like a feather
Mattress. Rest tonight and tomorrow
In the room next to mine
Tomorrow when you're feeling recovered
I have a proposition to put to you –
It involves going back. A spasm crossed
The wounds, a few drops of blood fell
On the floor. No, not that, my son
But to show there's no misunderstanding between us
Remember the last dark words and the sky.
The angels gagged me then by my orders in case
I intervened. Just to see a few friends
Walk round a bit like happier times
Be in their rooms without locks. Console them
Show yourself to the ones who seemed sorry.
The angels will take care of the stone.

Elizabeth Smither

Questions About Angels

Of all the questions you might want to ask
about angels, the only one you ever hear
is how many can dance on the head of a pin.

No curiosity about how they pass the eternal time
besides circling the Throne chanting in Latin
or delivering a crust of bread to a hermit on earth
or guiding a boy and girl across a rickety wooden bridge.

Do they fly through God's body and come out singing?
Do they swing like children from the hinges
of the spirit world saying their names backwards and forwards?
Do they sit alone in little gardens changing colors?

What about their sleeping habits, the fabric of their robes,
their diet of unfiltered divine light?
What goes on inside their luminous heads? Is there a wall
these tall presences can look over and see hell?

If an angel fell off a cloud, would he leave a hole
in a river and would the hole float along endlessly
filled with the silent letters of every angelic word?

If an angel delivered the mail, would he arrive
in a blinding rush of wings or would he just assume
the appearance of the regular mailman and
whistle up the driveway reading the postcards?

No, the medieval theologians control the court.
The only question you ever hear is about
the little dance floor on the head of a pin
where halos are meant to converge and drift invisibly.

It is designed to make us think in millions,
billions, to make us run out of numbers and collapse
into infinity, but perhaps the answer is simply one:
one female angel dancing alone in her stocking feet,
a small jazz combo working in the background.

She sways like a branch in the wind, her beautiful
eyes closed, and the tall thin bassist leans over
to glance at his watch because she has been dancing
forever, and now it is very late, even for musicians.

Billy Collins

Angel with a violin,
from a 13th century missal

A Blackbird Singing

It seems wrong that out of this bird,
Black, bold, a suggestion of dark
Places about it, there yet should come
Such rich music, as though the notes'
Ore were changed to a rare metal
At one touch of that bright bill.

You have heard it often, alone at your desk
In a green April, your mind drawn
Away from its work by sweet disturbance
Of the mild evening outside your room.

A slow singer, but loading each phrase
With history's overtones, love, joy
And grief learned by his dark tribe
In other orchards and passed on
Instinctively as they are now,
But fresh always with new tears.

R S Thomas

Raptor

You have made God small,
setting him astride
a pipette or a retort
studying the bubbles,
absorbed in an experiment
that will come to nothing.

I think of him rather
as an enormous owl
abroad in the shadows,
brushing me sometimes
with his wing so the blood
in my veins freezes, able

to find his way from one
soul to another because
he can see in the dark.
I have heard him crooning
to himself, so that almost
I could believe in angels,

those feathered overtones
in love's rafters, I have heard
him scream, too, fastening
his talons in his great
adversary, or in some lesser
denizen, maybe, like you or me.

R S Thomas

The Diary of an Old Soul

Sometimes, hard-trying, it seems I cannot pray –
For doubt, and pain, and anger, and all strife.
Yet some poor half-fledged prayer-bird from the nest
May fall, flit, fly, perch – crouch in the bowery breast
Of the large, nation-healing tree of life; –
Moveless there sit through all the burning day,
And on my heart at night a fresh leaf cooling lay.

My harvest withers. Health, my means to live –
All things seem rushing straight into the dark.
But the dark still is God. I would not give
The smallest silver-piece to turn the rush
Backward or sideways. Am I not a spark
Of him who is the light? – Fair hope doth flush
My east. – Divine success – Oh, hush and hark!

Thy will be done. I yield up everything.
"The life is more than meat" – then more than health;
"The body more than raiment" – then than wealth;
The hairs I made not, thou art numbering.
Thou art my life – I the brook, thou the spring.
Because thine eyes are open, I can see;
Because thou art thyself, 'tis therefore I am me.

George MacDonald

Advent

Bright in the night
a sudden appearing flame
trembles in the draught.
Uncertain at first,
its gasping breath
flickers, gathers strength,
and pushes back
the blackness;
corners of a room
take shape.
Soothed by its softness,
we are drawn
to the candle's
round, all-seeing light.

Sharp and insistent voices
dull to a murmur.
Jangling colours fade
to sand-ribbed shadows
on a falling tide.

Shadows that crowded
around us, conspiring
in our doubtful ears,
looming over our upraised
arms,
now sidle away, cowering;
overwhelmed by the love
that chases dark from light;
the love that dares to
call my name.

Alan Bing

103

Wenceslas

The King's Cook had cooked for the King a Christmas Pie,

wherein the Swan,
once bride of the river,
half of for ever,
six Cygnets circling her,
lay scalded, plucked, boned, parboiled,
salted, peppered, gingered, oiled;

and harboured the Heron
whose grey shadow she'd crossed
as it stood witness,
grave as a Priest,
on the riverbank

Now the Heron's breast was martyred with Cloves.

Inside the Heron inside the Swan –
in a greased cradle, pastry-sealed –
a Common Crane,
gutted and trussed,
smeared with Cicely, Lavender, Rose,
was stuffed with a buttered, saffroned
golden Goose.

Within the Goose,
perfumed with Fruits, was a Duck,
and jammed in the Duck, a Pheasant,
embalmed in Honey
from Bees
who'd perused
the blossoms of Cherry trees.

Spring in deep midwinter;
a year in a pie;
a Guinea-Fowl in a Pheasant;
a Teal in a Fowl.

Nursed in the Teal
Partridge, purse to a Plover;
a Plover, glove to a Quail;
and caught in the mitt of the Quail,
a Lark –
a green Olive stoppered its beak.

The Christmas Pie
for the good King, Wenceslas,
was seasoned with Sage, Rosemary, Thyme;
and a living Robin sang through a hole in its crust.

Pot-herbs to accompany this;
Roasted Chestnuts, Red Cabbage,
Celery, Carrots, Colly-flowre,
each borne aloft by a Page
into the Hall,
where the Pie steamed on a table
in front of the fire;

and to flow at the feast,
mulled Wine, fragrant
with Nutmeg, Cinnamon, Mace,
with Grains of Paradise.
The Lords and Ladies
sat at their places, candlelight
on their festive faces.

Up in the Minstrels' Gallery,
the King's Musicians tuned the Lute
to the Flute
to the Pipe
to the Shawm, the Gemshorn, the Harp,
to the Dulcimer
to the Psaltery;
and the Drum was a muffled heart
like an imminent birth
and the Tambourine was percussion as mirth.

Then a blushing Boy stood to trill
of how the Beasts, by some good spell,
in their crude stable began to tell
the gifts they gave Emmanuel.

Holly, Ivy, Mistletoe,
shredded Silver,
hung from the rafters

and the King's Fool
pranced beneath
five red Apples,
one green Pear,
which danced in the air.

Snow at the window twirled;
and deep, crisp, even,

covered the fields
where a fox and a vixen curled in a den
as the Moon scowled
at the cold, bold, gold glare of an Owl.

Also there,
out where the frozen stream
lay nailed to the ground,
was a prayer
drifting as human breath,
as the ghost of words,
in a dark wood,
yearning to be
Something
Understood.

But Heaven was only old light
and the frost was cruel
where a poor, stooped man
went gathering fuel.

A miracle then,

fanfared in,
that the King in red robes, silver crown,
glanced outside
from his wooden throne
to see the Pauper
stumble, shiver,

and sent a Page to fetch him
Hither.

Then Wenceslas sat the poor man down,
poured Winter's Wine,
and carved him a sumptuous slice
of the Christmas Pie ...
as prayers hope You would, and I.

Carol Ann Duffy

King's feast, Bayeux Tapestry, 11th century

Rivers Run into the Sea

The words of the Preacher, the son of David, king in Jerusalem.

Vanity of vanities, saith the Preacher, vanity of vanities; all is vanity.

What profit hath a man of all his labour which he taketh under the sun?

One generation passeth away, and another generation cometh: but the earth abideth for ever.

The sun also ariseth, and the sun goeth down, and hasteth to his place where he arose.

The wind goeth toward the south, and turneth about unto the north; it whirleth about continually, and the wind returneth again according to his circuits.

All the rivers run into the sea; yet the sea is not full; unto the place from whence the rivers come, thither they return again.

All things are full of labour; man cannot utter it: the eye is not satisfied with seeing, nor the ear filled with hearing.

The thing that hath been, it is that which shall be; and that which is done is that which shall be done: and there is no new thing under the sun.

King Solomon, *Ecclesiastes*

King James Bible

V. Dying

It seems to me that the present life of man on earth is like the swift flight of a single sparrow through the banqueting hall where you are sitting at dinner on a winter's day with your counsellors. In the midst there is a comforting fire to warm the hall. Outside, the storms of winter rain or snow are raging. This sparrow flies swiftly in through one door of the hall, and out through another. While he is inside, he is safe from the winter storms, but after a few moments of comfort, he vanishes from sight into the wintry world from which he came. So man appears on earth for a little while – but of what went before this life, or what follows, we know nothing.

Venerable Bede

Where We Are
(after Bede)

A man tears a chunk of bread off the brown loaf,
then wipes the gravy from his plate. Around him
at the long table, friends fill their mouths
with duck and roast pork, fill their cups from
pitchers of wine. Hearing a high twittering, the man

looks to see a bird – black with a white patch
beneath its beak – flying the length of the hall,
having flown in by a window over the door. As straight
as a taut string, the bird flies beneath the roofbeams,
as firelight flings its shadow against the ceiling.

The man pauses – one hand holds the bread, the other
rests upon the table – and watches the bird, perhaps
a swift, fly toward the window at the far end of the room.
He begins to point it out to his friends, but one is
telling hunting stories, as another describes the best way

to butcher a pig. The man shoves the bread in his mouth,
then slaps his hand down hard on the thigh of the woman
seated beside him, squeezes his fingers to feel the firm
muscles and tendons beneath the fabric of her dress.
A huge dog snores on the stone hearth by the fire.

From the window comes the clicking of pine needles
blown against it by an October wind. A half moon
hurries along behind scattered clouds, while the forest
of black spruce and bare maple and birch surrounds
the long hall the way a single rock can be surrounded

by a river. This is where we are in history – to think
the table will remain full; to think the forest will
remain where we have pushed it; to think our bubble of
good fortune will save us from the night – a bird flies in
from the dark, flits across a lighted hall and disappears.

Stephen Dobyns

Day Trip

Two women, seventies, hold hands
on the edge of Essex,
hair in strong nets,
shrieked laughter echoing gulls
as shingle sucks from under feet
easing in brine.

There must be an unspoken point
when the sea feels like
their future. No longer paddling,
ankles submerge in lace,
in satin ripple.

They do not risk their balance
for the shimmering of ships
at the horizon's sweep
as, thigh deep, they inch on
fingers splayed, wrists bent,
learning to walk again.

Carole Satyamurti

Old Woman

So much she caused she cannot now account for
As she stands watching day return, the cool
Walls of the house moving towards the sun.
She puts some flowers in a vase and thinks
    "There is not much I can arrange
In here and now, but flowers are suppliant

As children never were. And love is now
A flicker of memory, my body is
My own entirely. When I lie at night
I gather nothing now into my arms,
    No child or man, and where I live
Is what remains when men and children go."

Yet she owns more than residue of lives
That she has marked and altered. See how she
Warns time from too much touching her possessions
By keeping flowers fed, by polishing
    Her fine old silver. Gratefully
She sees her own glance printed on grandchildren.

Thawing the curtains back and opening windows
Every morning now, she feels her years
Grow less and less. Time puts no burden on
Her now she does not need to measure it.
    It is acceptance she arranges
And her own life she places in the vase.

Elizabeth Jennings

Deaths of Flowers

I would if I could choose
Age and die outwards as a tulip does;
Not as this iris drawing in, in-coiling
Its complex strange taut inflorescence, willing
Itself a bud again – though all achieved is
No more than a clenched sadness,

The tears of gum not flowing.
I would choose the tulip's reckless way of going;
Whose petals answer light, altering by fractions
From closed to wide, from one through many perfections,
Til wrecked, flamboyant, strayed beyond recall,
Like flakes of fire they piecemeal fall.

E J Scovell

Nicholas Ferrar

You died the hour you used to rise for prayer.
In that rich hush beneath all other sounds,
You rose at one and took the midnight air
Rising and falling on the wings and rounds
Of psalms and silence. The December stars
Shine clear above the Giddings, promised light
For those who dwell in darkness. Morning stirs
The household. From the folds of sleep, the late
Risers wake to find you gone, and pray
Through pain and grief to bless your journey home;
Those last glad steps in the right good old way
Up to the door where Love will bid you welcome.
Love draws us too, towards your grave and haven
We greet you at the very gate of Heaven.

Malcolm Guite

Late Snow

An end. Or a beginning.
Snow had fallen again and covered
the old dredge and blackened mush
with a gleaming pelt; but high up there
in the sycamore top, Thaw
Thaw, the rooks cried,
sentinel by ruined nests.

Water was slacking into runnels
from drifts and pitted snowbacks,
dripping from the gutter and ragged
icicle fringes. Snow paused
in the shining embrace of bushes,
waiting in ledged curds and bluffs
to tumble into soft explosions.

And suddenly your absence
drove home its imperatives like frost,
and I ran to the high field
clumsily as a pregnant woman
to tread our names in blemished
brilliant drifts; because the time we have
is shrinking away like snow.

M R Peacocke

Stanzas

Subjoined to the Yearly Bill of Mortality of the Parish of All Saints,
Northampton, for the year 1790

Despise not my good counsel - Buchanan

He who sits from day to day
Where the prison'd lark is hung,
Heedless of his loudest lay,
Hardly knows that he has sung.

Where the watchman in his round
Nightly lifts his voice on high,
None, accustom'd to the sound,
Wakes the sooner for his cry.

So your verse-man I, and clerk,
Yearly in my song proclaim
Death at hand – yourselves his mark –
And the foe's unerring aim.

Duly at my time I come,
Publishing to all aloud –
Soon the grave must be your home,
And your only suit, a shroud.

But the monitory strain,
Oft repeated in your ears,
Seems to sound too much in vain,
Wins no notice, wakes no fears.

Can a truth, by all confess'd
Of such magnitude and weight,
Grow, by being oft impress'd,
Trivial as a parrot's prate?

Pleasure's call attention wins,
Hear it often as we may;
New as ever seem our sins,
Though committed every day.

Death and Judgement, heaven and hell –
These alone, so often heard,
No more move us than the bell,
When some stranger is interr'd.

O then, ere the turf or tomb
Cover us from ev'ry eye,
Spirit of instruction, come,
Make us learn that we must die.

William Cowper

Shadows

And if tonight my soul may find her peace
in sleep, and sink in good oblivion,
and in the morning wake like a new-opened flower
then I have been dipped again in God, and new-created.

And if, as weeks go round, in the dark of the moon
my spirit darkens and goes out, and soft strange gloom
pervades my movements and my thoughts and words
then I shall know that I am walking still
with God, we are close together now the moon's in shadow.

And if, as autumn deepens and darkens
I feel the pain of falling leaves, and stems that break in storms
and trouble and dissolution and distress
and then the softness of deep shadows folding,
folding around my soul and spirit, around my lips
so sweet, like a swoon, or more like the drowse of a low, sad song
singing darker than the nightingale, on, on to the solstice
and the silence of short days, the silence of the year, the shadow,
then I shall know that my life is moving still
with the dark earth, and drenched
with the deep oblivion of earth's lapse and renewal.

And if, in the changing phases of man's life
I fall in sickness and in misery
my wrists seem broken and my heart seems dead
and strength is gone, and my life
is only the leavings of a life:

and still, among it all, snatches of lovely oblivion, and snatches
of renewal
odd, wintry flowers upon the withered stem, yet new, strange flowers
such as my life has not brought forth before, new blossoms of me

then I must know that still
I am in the hands of the unknown God,
he is breaking me down to his own oblivion
to send me forth on a new morning, a new man.

                                                    D H Lawrence

In Memoriam

Private D. Sutherland killed in action on the German trench, May 16th 1916, and the others who died.

So you were David's father,
And he was your only son,
And the new-cut peats are rotting
And the work is left undone,
Because of an old man weeping,
Just an old man in pain,
For David, his son David,
That will not come again.

Oh, the letters he wrote you,
And I can see them still,
Not a word of the fighting,
But just the sheep on the hill
And how you should get the crops in
Ere the year get stormier,
And the Bosches have got his body,
And I was his officer.

You were only David's father,
But I had fifty sons
When we went up in the evening
Under the arch of the guns,
And we came back at twilight -
O God! I heard them call
To me for help and pity
That could not help at all.

Oh, never will I forget you,
My men that trusted me,
More my sons than your fathers',
For they could only see
The little helpless babies
And the young men in their pride.

They could not see you dying,
And hold you while you died.

Happy and young and gallant,
They saw their first-born go,
But not the strong limbs broken
And the beautiful men brought low,
The piteous writhing bodies,
They screamed "Don't leave me, sir",
For they were only your fathers
But I was your officer.

Ewart Alan Mackintosh

(killed in action 21st November 1917 aged 24)

Lochan

for Jean Johnstone

When all this is over I mean
to travel north, by the high

drove roads and cart tracks
probably in June,

with the gentle dog-roses
flourishing beside me. I mean

to find among the thousands
scattered in that land

a certain quiet lochan,
where water lilies rise

like small fat moons,
and tied among the reeds,

underneath a rowan,
a white boat waits.

Kathleen Jamie

After A Journey

I come to interview a Voiceless ghost;
Whither, O whither will its whim now draw me?
Up the cliff, down, till I'm lonely, lost,
And the unseen waters' soliloquies awe me.
Where you will next be there's no knowing,
Facing round about me everywhere,
With your nut-coloured hair,
And gray eyes, and rose-flush coming and going.

Yes: I have re-entered your olden haunts at last;
Through the years, through the dead scenes I have tracked you;
What have you now found to say of our past -
Viewed across the dark space wherein I have lacked you?
Summer gave us sweets, but autumn wrought division?
Things were not lastly as firstly well
With us twain, you tell?
But all's closed now, despite Time's derision.

I see what you are doing: you are leading me on
To the spots we knew when we haunted here together,
The waterfall, above which the mist-bow shone
At the then fair hour in the then fair weather,
And the cave just under, with a voice still so hollow
That it seems to call out to me from forty years ago,
When you were all aglow,
And not the thin ghost that I now fraily follow!

Ignorant of what there is flitting here to see,
The waked birds preen and the seals flop lazily,
Soon you will have, Dear, to vanish from me,
For the stars close their shutters and the dawn whitens hazily.
Trust me, I mind not, though Life lours,
The bringing of me here; nay, bring me here again!
I am just the same as when
Our days were a joy, and our paths through flowers.

Thomas Hardy

Beyond the Headlines

Then I saw the wild geese flying
In fair formation to their bases in Inchicore
And I knew that these wings would outwear the wings of war
And a man's simple thoughts outlive the day's loud lying.
Don't fear, don't fear, I said to my soul.
The Bedlam of Time is an empty bucket rattled,
'Tis you who will say in the end who best battles.
Only they who fly home to God have flown at all.

Patrick Kavanagh

Waterbirds

Out of the huge sadness of the Iliad
(I was reading Book Fifteen when you died)
Waterbirds are calling – barnacle geese,
Grey herons and long-necked whooper swans.
Waterbirds in flight over a water-meadow,
Honking, settling in front of one another,
Proud of their feather-power – taking me back
To the camogie pitch where your heart failed.
Waterbirds are calling – barnacle geese,
Grey herons and long-necked whooper swans.

Michael Longley

Murmuration

After the funeral we drove down to the Levels, parked
and walked the last bit arm in arm
to where you thought the starlings would be.

The sky was purple with the leaving sun.
All we could hear was the patter of birds' wings above,
see the flock flickering tip to tip over the reedbeds,

and it was as if the world's words had come to an end,
each flight a jumble of inky characters
that danced and wavered in the purple sky

then plunged down joyful with the grieving sun.
We stood still and watched it, the end of the earth,
flushing with cold and wonder and sadness;

silent by instinct we waited together,
shoulder to shoulder, mother and daughter,
feeling the grief of the last dance, of rising the gladness.

Katy Morgan

Healing

Sick wards. The sailed beds
becalmed. The nurses tack
hither and fro. The chloroform
breeze rises and falls.
Hospitals are their own
weather. The temperatures
have no relation
to the world outside. The surgeons,
those cunning masters
of navigation, follow
their scalpels' compass through
hurricanes of pain to a calm
harbour. Somewhere far down
in the patient's darkness,
where faith died, like a graft
or a transplant prayer
gets to work, repairing
the soul's tissue, leading
the astonished self between
twin pillars, where life's angels
stand wielding their bright swords of flame.

R S Thomas

Exile

Yes, it is a beautiful country,
the streams in the winding valley,
the knows and the birches,
and beautiful the mountain's bare shoulder
and the calm brows of the hills,
but it is not my country,
and in my heart there is a hollow place always.

And there is no way to go back –
maybe the miles indeed, but the years never.

Winding are the roads that we choose,
and inexorable is life,
driving us, it seems, like cattle
farther and farther away from what we remember.

But when we shall come at last
to God, who is our Home and Country,
there will be no more road stretching before us
and no more need to go back.

Evangeline Paterson

The Dead

The dead are always looking down on us, they say.
while we are putting on our shoes or making a sandwich,
they are looking down through the glass bottom boats of heaven
as they row themselves slowly through eternity.

They watch the tops of our heads moving below on earth,
and when we lie down in a field or on a couch,
drugged perhaps by the hum of a long afternoon,
they think we are looking back at them,
which makes them lift their oars and fall silent
and wait, like parents, for us to close our eyes.

Billy Collins

Death, be not proud

Death, be not proud, though some have called thee
Mighty and dreadful, for thou art not so;
For those whom thou think'st thou dost overthrow
Die not, poor Death, nor yet canst thou kill me.
From rest and sleep, which but thy pictures be,
Much pleasure; then from thee much more must flow,
And soonest our best men with thee do go,
Rest of their bones, and soul's delivery.
Thou art slave to fate, chance, kings, and desperate men,
And dost with poison, war, and sickness dwell,
And poppy or charms can make us sleep as well
And better than thy stroke; why swell'st thou then?
One short sleep past, we wake eternally
And death shall be no more; Death, thou shalt die.

John Donne

A New Creation

All around us we observe a pregnant creation. The difficult times of pain throughout the world are simply birth pangs. But it's not only around us; it's within us. The Spirit of God is arousing us within. We're also feeling the birth pangs. These sterile and barren bodies of ours are yearning for full deliverance. That is why waiting does not diminish us, any more than waiting diminishes a pregnant mother. We are enlarged in the waiting. We, of course, don't see what is enlarging us. But the longer we wait, the larger we become, and the more joyful our expectancy.

St Paul
Letter to the Romans, chapter 8
The Message

Resurrection, by Luca Signorelli (1445-1523)

Resurrection

Is it true that after this life of ours we shall one day be awakened
by a terrifying clamour of trumpets?
Forgive me God, but I console myself
that the beginning and resurrection of all of us dead
will simply be announced by the crowing of the cock.

After that we'll remain lying down a while...
The first to get up
will be Mother... We'll hear her
quietly laying the fire,
quietly putting the kettle on the stove
and cosily taking the teapot out of the cupboard.
We'll be home once more.

Vladimir Holan

Day Dream

One day people will touch and talk perhaps, easily,
And loving be natural as breathing and warm as sunlight,;
And people will untie themselves, as string is unknotted,
Unfold and yawn and stretch and spread their fingers,
Unfurl, uncurl like seaweed returned to the sea,

And work will be simple and swift as a seagull flying,
And play will be casual and quiet as a seagull settling;
And the clocks will stop, and no one will wonder or care or notice,
And people will smile without reason, even in winter, even in the rain.

A S J Tessimond

Poetry acknowledgements

Works by the following poets are reproduced by kind permission of the authors, their representatives or publishers:

Akhmatova, Anna: from *Selected Poems*, translated by DM Thomas, reproduced by permission of The Random House Group Ltd.

Amichai, Yehuda: from *The Selected Poetry of Yehuda Amichai*, edited and translated by Chana Bloch and Stephen Mitchell, © 2013 by Chana Bloch and Stephen Mitchell. Published by the University of California Press.

Ashworth, Anne: by permission of the author

Bing, Alan: by permission of the author

Bishop, Elizabeth: from *Complete Poems*, published by Vintage and reproduced by permission of The Random House Group Ltd.

Cardenal, Ernesto: "On Lake Nicaragua", translated by Robert Pring-Mill, from *Apocalypse and Other Poems*, copyright ©1977 by Ernesto Cardenal and Robert Pring-Mill. Reprinted by permission of New Directions Publishing Corp.

Collins, Billy: from *Questions About Angels*, Pittsburgh Press 1991. All rights are controlled by the University of Pittsburgh Press.

Cottrell, Stephen: by permission of the author

David, King: from the *New Revised Standard Version Bible*, Anglicized Edition, copyright © 1989, 1995 by the Division of Christian Education of the National Council of the Churches of Christ in the United States of America. Used by permission. All rights reserved.

De Bernières, Louis, from *The Dust that Falls from Dreams*, published by Vintage. Reproduced with permission from The Random House Group Ltd.

Dobyns, Stephen: by permission of the author

Duffy, Carol Ann: 'Wenceslas' from *Collected Poems*, Picador 2015, © Carol Ann Duffy. Reproduced by permission of the author c/o Rogers, Coleridge & White Ltd, 20 Powis Mews, London W11 1JN. 'The Virgin Punishing the Infant' from *New Selected Poems*, Picador 2004, © Carol Ann Duffy. Reproduced by permission of the author c/o Rogers, Coleridge & White Ltd, 20 Powis Mews, London W11 1JN.

Fanthorpe, UA: from *Neck Verse*, Peterloo Poets 1992, by permission of RV Bailey

Graves, Robert: from *Complete Poems in One Volume*, Carcanet Press 2000, by permission of Carcanet Press Limited, Manchester

Graham, WS: 'To Alexander Graham,' reproduced by permission of Rosalind Mudaliar, the estate of W.S. Graham.

Works by the following are in the public domain and freely available in published collections or online:

Browning, Robert (1812-1899)
Bunyan, John (1628-1688)
Cavafy, Constantine (1863-1933)
Clare, John (1793-1864)
Cowper, William (1731-1800)
Donne, John (1572-1631)
Hardy, Thomas (1840-1928)
Herbert, George (1593-1633)
Housman, AE (1859-1936)
Lawrence, DH (1885-1930)
Longfellow, Henry Wadsworth (1807-1882)
MacDonald, George (1824-1905)
Mackintosh, Ewart Alan (1893-1917)
Mew, Charlotte (1869-1928)
Shakespeare, William (1564-1616)
Solomon, King: 'Song of Songs', from *The King James Bible*
Thomas, Edward (1878-1917)
Yeats, William Butler (1865-1939)

Prose extracts are taken from the following works:

Baker, JA: *The Peregrine*, Penguin 1967
Bede, The Venerable: *Ecclesiastical History of the English People*, OUP 1990
Buechner, Frederick: *Now and Then*, Harper & Row 1983
Dillard, Annie: *The Writing Life*, Harper Perennial 1989
Hardy, Robert: *Longbow*, Patrick Stephens 1956
Hoskins, WS: *The Making of the English Landscape*, Hodder & Stoughton 1955
Joyce, James: *Portrait of the Artist as a Young Man*, Penguin Classics 2000
Mayne, Michael: *Learning to Dance*, DLT 2001
Scruton, Roger: *The Soul of the World*, Princeton University Press 2014
Spufford, Francis: *Unapologetic*, Faber & Faber 2012
Thomas, RS: 'A Thicket in Lleyn', in *Britain: A World by Itself*, ed Franklin Perring, Aurum Press 1984

Image acknowledgements

If you liked this collection...

Try *Distilling Life: Poems for Reflection and Meditation*, edited by Alison Morgan and Martin Cavender, ReSource 2012 – available from www.alisonmorgan.co.uk, or on Amazon.

Something Understood is published by The Mathetes Trust. Copies can be ordered from our website www.mathetestrust.org.